The Secret of Happiness

For Mice and Other People

The Laws of Nature
Rules for a Successful Life

Sandra Jantzen - Robert Jansen - Andrea Ludwig

Index

Stories touch and connect young and old alike. They create pictures that help us to share the knowledge of past generations.
"The Secret of Happiness" talks about the laws of Nature. They've existed for thousands of years and are more relevant than ever before. Always showing respect for mankind, animals and plants enables our survival. The story of the mice brothers Carl and Johnny describes the rules of the game for a successful life.

By living life as an adventure, Carl and Johnny experience the realization of their dreams. They stumble into a world of challenges and possibilities. They overcame a crisis and resistance to outperform themselves.

Sandra Jantzen wrote the heart-warming adventures and stories about the mice brothers. Robert Jansen, a former farmer, delivers the details and factual information concerning agriculture. Andrea Ludwig manages the overall project and ensures a successful outcome.

Our collaboration in this project shows what a team can create with ease. What's possible when everybody brings in his or her strengths to a project. With a lot of pleasure and verve we realized this book within a few weeks. One person alone would have never been able to do it.

All three of us have one mission. We stand for a new kind of entrepreneurship. We want to encourage people to live their own dreams and we want to show that you can earn a living by doing the things you love to do. Our vision is for respectful cooperation from which everyone benefits. We stand for greater humanity in business and for connections in which everybody wins.

Sandra Jantzen - Robert Jansen - Andrea Ludwig

It is Tuesday. The lunch break is over and the afternoon class is just starting. The topic of the class is: "What will I be when I grow up?" Luke stands in front of the chalkboard and talks about his dream job. He wants to become the president of a large chocolate mill. He loves chocolate, but they don't have chocolate very often at home. His parents earn very little money. He tells the class, that as the boss of the chocolate mill, he would give the children chocolate once a week to make them happy.

Bobby, who is sitting in the last row, almost fell out of his chair laughing. "Go on dreaming, Luke! How do you plan to become a boss? Forget about that! To do this, you will need money. A lot of money! You are a poor boy, you don't have any money!"
Luke is frightened. He wishes the ground would open and swallow him up. His family really doesn't have a lot of money, but is he poor? Is that a reason not to be able to work in his dream job? There is turmoil in the class, but he doesn't realize it. Completely dazed, he sits down again. His teacher says some encouraging words to him, but he cannot hear them over his doubts.

After school, he goes home with his head down. He doesn't want to see or hear anybody. When he opens the door, his grandpa Francis approaches him. He is always there at noon, when Luke's parents are working. Grandpa Francis sees Luke's depressed face.
"What happened to you?" Luke doesn't answer.

"Come here." Grandpa Francis sits on the chair in the hall and picks up his grandson to place him on his lap. A tear drops out of Luke's eye.
"What happened?"
Sobbing, Luke tells his grandpa everything. When he is ready, he asks: "Grandpa, is it really not possible for me to become the president of a chocolate-mill?"
Grandpa Francis wipes the tears from Luke's cheeks and says: "Let me tell you a story."

***

Once upon a time ...

... in a mice-land far away behind the mountains and beyond the seas, between green hills and mellow meadows, there was a small valley known as Happiness. The mice living in that village were happy and had no worries. Everyone enjoyed life, the sun, the wind and the smell of the meadows and flowers. Even storms and bad weather couldn't cloud their mood. How was this possible? It was a well-kept secret...

Far away, the mice brothers Carl and Johnny lived in the big city called Mousetropolis, where the buildings leaned like great grey giants against one another, blocking the sunlight from shining into the streets.
Every day, the brothers wandered through the neighborhood looking for food. They found just enough to keep them from dying of hunger. Sometimes they found a piece of bread, or an apple that fell off a truck. When they were fortunate, there was an open trash container out

behind a popular restaurant. They only needed to climb into it and pick the finest treats. But today they weren't having any luck. The trash bin was locked. So they kept looking.

Carl stopped in front of a kiosk . He gazed at the magazines with the pictures of all of the most successful mice in the country. Posing in suits and with important looks, they smiled into the camera. They changed the country and won prizes.

As Carl pushed his nose against the window of the kiosk, his eyes grew bigger and bigger. "Someday I will be on the front-page of one of those magazines", he exclaimed. "Then I will have so much to eat that I will never be hungry again!"

Completely lit up, he turned. Immediately, his joy went away when he saw Johnny, who said angrily: "Don‘t start talking that nonsense again! How would you do that? We are busy all day long. What else should we do? Let‘s go!“

"I only thought...“ Carl trotted disappointedly behind Johnny. He looked back to the magazines. Some day, he would make it!

They returned home completely exhausted and fell into their beds that evening. They didn‘t even notice the envelope that lay on the floor.

The next day dawned sunny. Despite the shadows, rays of sunlight danced through the room. They tickled Carl‘s nose. Slowly he rubbed his eyes awake. As he was stretching, his glance fell on the floor. Was he dreaming or did he see a real letter? Who would have written a letter to them? Nobody knows them here.

With a big hop, he jumped out of bed and opened the envelope. His eyes flew over the paper. There was something written about an uncle in a village called Happiness. The handwriting told an interesting story. Their long-lost Uncle Theodore was old and couldn‘t harvest his crops on his own. He wanted to know if they could come and help him.

Carl suddenly remembered that when he and Johnny were kids, they visited this uncle at his farm every holiday. There were a lot of things to do there: driving the tractor, milking the cows, harvesting the cabbage, feeding the chickens and playing with the children of the village. A picture came into his mind of when they sat at the table with the whole family, in front of a lavish meal. He could not remember a single day on which they needed to worry about not having food on the table.

Now, he wanted to know for sure why his uncle was writing. He read the whole letter again, word for word. That was the solution! His heart jumped for joy. Shouting with excitement, he went to Johnny‘s bed and shook him until he woke up. Johnny grumbled: "Why are you making so much noise? I want to sleep!“
"I know how we can never have to worry about food again!“
"Okay", Johnny sat up slowly.
Carl waved the letter wildly in front of Johnny‘s nose: "This is the solution!“
"A letter?“, asked Johnny.
"Yes, it's a special letter. Uncle Theodore wrote it.“
Then he started to explain. He didn‘t leave out any details. "Imagine, every day we would have enough food and those green meadows and the fresh air and...“
In the meantime, Carl‘s enthusiasm jumped over to Johnny. He laughed: "Ok, ok. You are totally stoked. Hand me the letter, please.“
Carl gave the letter to Johnny. With big eyes Carl watched how Johnny read the letter. When he was finished, he laid the paper down.
"And?“, Carl asked, full of anticipation.
"Hm", Johnny stroked his chin, "I have no clue if it is the right thing, but I say we travel to Happiness!“
"Yeahhh!“ Carl wrapped his arms around Johnny‘s neck.

So, they packed their suitcases and took the train to go to the valley behind the mountains and beyond the seas.

During the whole journey, Carl was talking about the thick cabbage. He wanted to become the super cabbage farmer. That shouldn‘t be too difficult. He would have the biggest cabbage ever. Then he would appear on the front pages of the magazines and would never be hungry again. He talked about every cabbage-recipe in the world. At least Johnny thought so. He got almost a cabbage growing out his ear.

The First Lesson

Finally, they reached the small railway station of Happiness. Uncle Theodore was already waiting for them. He stood there on the platform, leaning on his cane. He wore his blue overalls and a green jacket. Exactly as he used to do when the boys were small.
"Hi, Uncle Theodore!", Carl shouted.
"Hello, Johnny and Carl", Uncle Theodore answered. "You both grew very tall.“
"It has been a while since we stayed here the last time.“
"That‘s true. It is so nice that you are here.“
They hugged one another and went to the parking lot. Uncle Theodore still drove his old horse-drawn buggy. They loaded up the luggage and started down the road.
They enjoyed the blue skies, as the sun was shining on the green hills and the juicy meadows. They drove along a small avenue with big trees.

The leaves rustled as if they said 'hello‘ to the arrivals. At the end of the avenue, they reached Uncle Theodore‘s farm. Everything was still in its place: At the left was the garage for the machines and in front of this was the barn, where the animals curiously looked out. At the right stood the house. Every window still had a flower-box with bright red cranesbills in front.

They got out of the cart and Carl and Johnny stood there, their eyes wide open. They had almost forgotten how beautiful this place was.
"It would be best if you took your luggage to your rooms. Do you still know where to find them?“, Uncle Theodore said.
"Yes sir!“ The mice-brothers ran. Uncle Theodore shouted after them, "I‘ll prepare dinner. I think you are hungry after that long journey.“
What a perfect beginning, Carl thought and ran as quickly as he could to the house.
When they entered the kitchen, it smelled like cabbage and potatoes. Quickly Carl and Johnny sat at the table. Uncle Theodore cooked their favorite dish. They ate and told Uncle Theodore what they had experienced in past years. They ate until they were nearly bursting. Not even a pea would have had any space in their stomachs. They almost fell out of their chairs. Uncle Theodore laughed: "It is good that you liked the food.“
"That was the best meal I ever had!“ Johnny wiped his mouth. Carl rubbed his thick belly.
It was starting to get dark outside.
Uncle Theodore got serious, "I am glad that you are here. I really need your help. I am getting very weak. The harvest is coming up, the cabbage is

ready and the grain is also mature. The animals need to be looked after."
"We will help you. That‘s why we came", Carl said.
"That‘s good", said Uncle Theodore, "Here is your first task."
The mice brothers cocked their ears.
"Elsa, the cow, needs to have water and straw. You can find everything you need in the barn. I need to rest and I'll see you tomorrow morning."
"Ok. We‘ll do that. Sleep well", Johnny answered.
They cleared the table and dragged themselves and their full bellies to the barn.
Here it smelled of fresh hay and the animals. It was cozy and warm. The warmth made them sleepy. Carl stood in front of the straw and said "That looks very comfortable." He yawned.
"We could lay down and rest a while."
"We cannot do that. Uncle Theodore told us to give Elsa water and straw."
"Oh, only one minute. He will not even notice."
"I don‘t know." Johnny was unsure.
"Don‘t be a killjoy."
Johnny gave up. A small minute, that nobody would notice. So they lay down and went to sleep peacefully. They slept and slept and didn‘t hear Elsa mooing loudly. She was hungry and thirsty.

Carl and Johnny slept until the morning. They stretched and went into the house. They totally forgot about Elsa. Uncle Theodore was already waiting for them with breakfast. "Hey, did you have a good night‘s rest?" he asked. Both nodded. "Then let us first have breakfast."
"Do you have any of that delicious milk?", asked Carl.

"Today there is no milk", Uncle Theodore said calmly.
"Why not?", the boys asked.
"You didn't give Elsa straw and water last night. If Elsa doesn't feel good, she will not give any milk. If you want to milk her, you need to treat her well."
"We fell asleep.", Carl said, ashamed.
"Now you know what's important and in the future you will take very good care of Elsa."
"We will do that", said Johnny.

From this day on, Carl and Johnny were very attentive to Elsa. They made sure that Elsa always had enough water and straw. And Elsa rewarded them with a whole lot of good milk. Everybody was lucky.

The days passed by. Uncle Theodore showed them everything they needed to know for harvesting. They got up early in the morning and fell into bed late at night. Even if the sun was shining, or if it was raining, they didn't stop working. Uncle Theodore explained to them the way nature works, and how if you sowed, watered and fertilized your crops, you would be able to harvest them in the end. They accepted that and they were happy. They harvested the biggest cabbages and the golden grain from the fields. They didn't finish until they had everything in the big silos. Satisfied, they looked at the full stores. Uncle Theodore was very proud of the mice-boys. They did everything as he had showed them.

The Mystical Book

It was a grey day in December. Uncle Theodore knew his last hours were coming. He lay in bed and Carl and Johnny sat beside him. Carl wept a tear from the corner of his eye.

"Uncle Theodore, you are not so old yet."

Johnny said: "You cannot leave us alone. We have not yet learned all we need to know."

"I have taught you everything you need. Now you only need to follow my instructions." He drew out a big, leather-bound book with a big seal. "That's for you. In that book you will find the secret of Happiness. It is the knowledge of ancient times. It is passed from generation to generation. Now it is your task to heed it. He gave the book to Carl and Johnny. Johnny's paws shivered. He opened the book.

"The pages are empty!", he shouted out, very confused.

"When the time comes, you will see it." Then Uncle Theodore closed his eyes forever. He died a peaceful death. He knew the secret would be in good hands.

"The pages are empty?" Carl sniffed. He didn't know if he should be sad or angry. Why did their uncle give them an empty book? He browsed wildly through the book. All the pages were empty.

"What the crap?!", he called out. "What are we supposed to do with an empty book?" He threw the book in the corner.

They fell into a deep depression. What now? They didn't know how to go on, so they just waited.

Outside it was cold and dark. They only did the most important things, caring for the animals and living from the reserves.

One evening, Carl sat at the window. Outside it started to get dark. He saw the happy villagers who laughed and chatted. They enjoyed their lives. On Uncle Theodore's shelf, he found a book about success. It was about how to earn a lot of money while having fun. He only read a few pages. He didn't understand everything, but it sounded very interesting. He already saw himself on the cover of the famous magazines. Now, he only needed to have lots of fun. He jumped to his feet. "Now we are going to party", he called. Just then, the doorbell rang. Johnny got up from his chair and opened the door. Out there stood the rats of the town. They had heard that Carl and Johnny were doing so well now and wanted to visit them. Johnny didn't have much enthusiasm for them. He didn't like the rats. Carl however was glad to see the visitors. For him, the rats came just at the right time. So, they could have a party, a grain-party! With all the tasty grain in the silo.

"What do you think about that, Johnny?", asked Carl.
"I don't think that's such a good idea."
"Why not?"
"The winter is going to be long and we need to get through it with our provisions."
"Don't make such a fuss", one of the rats said.
"Exactly", said Carl, "Our silo is so huge. A little party wouldn't do any harm and the others in the village will also have fun."

"Let's leave that party-pooper and party on our own." With these words the rats dragged Carl out of the house into the direction of the silo. Johnny stayed in the room and calmed himself down. Surely, Carl would be careful. He decided to go to bed.

At midnight the party was in full swing. The rats stormed the silo and declared it a party-zone. They had a lot of fun. They laughed and glided down the golden grain-hills, they danced along the floor board and stuffed grains into their mouths. Carl had invited them to eat as much as they wanted to. Eventually, it was enough. They partied for hours and Carl was right in the middle. He was having the time of his life. Nobody realized how the grain-hills shrank and finally vanished completely. All that remained was a small heap of grain. They kept dancing.

Johnny woke up because of the noise. He trotted dozily to the silo. When he saw that it was empty, he suddenly awakened. He rubbed his eyes. Was he still dreaming? He pinched himself in the arm. "Ouch!" No, he was awake. And the silo was empty.

"Hey, Johnny!", Carl welcomed him. "Come on, party with us. There's lots of grain left." He turned and pointed into the wideness of the shed. Then he saw that it was empty. His jaw dropped, and he was paralyzed with fear.
"What did you do?", Johnny asked furiously.
"Oh no, I didn't want that. There was so much grain. Where is it now?" Carl nervously walked up

and down the silo. He searched in every corner. He walked as quickly as he could and stumbled over his feet. With a big thud, he fell on his belly. He slipped along the floor and stopped exactly in front of the last small pile of grain. He looked at it with big eyes. Was that all that remained? What had he done?

Uncle Theodore came into his mind. He had told them the story of the farmer and his seeds: It was in winter. The farmer and his family were very hungry. They wanted to eat the grain. But the farmer told them that they mustn't eat it, because if they did, they wouldn't have anything to sow in spring. If they couldn't sow, then next year the villagers wouldn't have any grain to make bread. The whole village would starve from hunger. He defended his seed with everything he had. Even when one of his children died, he didn‘t give the grain away. In the next spring he sowed the seed and at the end of the year the whole village had bread and didn‘t need to starve from hunger. Uncle Theodore said: "A farmer never eats his seed.“

Carl picked himself up slowly. In front of him lay the small pile of grain. Tears came into his eyes. He murmured: "Oh no, oh no.“ Very carefully he collected every tiny seed and pushed the small pile together. Protectively he laid himself on top. "Now I will pay attention so that none of the grains disappear.“
In the meantime the rats had all gone and left only an empty silo, a horrified Johnny and a sad Carl.
"We need to make the best out of it“, Johnny said and placed himself beside Carl.
"I will fix this“, Carl said.

Carl‘s Great Impatience

Spring came and the sun threw its first warming rays onto the countryside. Everything brightened and the people came out of their houses. The birds crossed the sky twittering. There was buzzing and vibration everywhere.

Much preparation started in the fields. It was the time to sow. Carl and Johnny were also in the fields. Carl was eagerly ploughing the ground. Forcefully, he broke the soil up to loosen it. He knew he had to carefully work the earth so that the plants could grow well. He imagined how he made the plants a nice home, in which they could feel comfortable. He tried hard. After all, he had something to fix.

The little seed they had had to grow well in an extraordinary way. They were lucky to have the cabbage seeds. They didn't eat them at the party.
They ridged channels and placed the seeds. Carefully they sowed and watered the seed.
"What do you think, how long will it take until it grows?", asked Carl.
Johnny answered: "I don't know. It will take some time."
"Hm, hopefully not too long", Carl murmured.
When they finished sowing, they took their equipment and went home. They were tired, but satisfied.

During the following days, Carl was always the first to be in the field. He wanted to see if something had already grown. Every day, he was disappointed, because nothing visible happened. Johnny said they had to be patient and continue the care every day, consistently. After one week Carl was fed up. How would they ever be rich? He decided to get to the bottom of the case. The next morning he went to the field and started to dig. He excavated some of the seeds. Most of them already had small roots. Ok, Carl thought, at least they started to move. So he planted them again. He didn't tell Johnny about it. Two weeks later, the first tender green leaves came into the light. Except at the place where Carl dug out the seed, almost everything was growing.

Johnny was wondering, "That‘s strange. We sow here like in the other places. Why doesn‘t the seed grow here?“
Carl was ashamed, "Probably a bird picked the seed out.“ He made an innocent face. Johnny watched him with suspicion.
"I don‘t believe that. Could it be that my brother had a finger in the pie?“
"You know", red-faced, Carl looked embarrassed at the floor, "I only wanted to see if it was growing and so I dug out the seed.“
Johnny nodded his head, "You always have such crazy ideas. This is no different than if I were to shake you at night to see if you were already sleeping.“
"I didn‘t know that.“
"Ok, let us just go on. We need to weed.“

So, they weeded for several hours. Suddenly, an idea popped into Carl‘s mind. Perhaps the cabbage grew quicker when you pulled it a little bit. He saw that Johnny was busy and wouldn‘t notice him. He needed to try it at once. Carefully, he pulled. 'I think it‘s going to work', Carl thought gladly. The leaves appeared already longer. He pulled again. Plop! Suddenly he held the whole plant in his hand. Dumbfounded, he looked at the little plant. " Bugger!" Quickly he peered to Johnny. He didn‘t realize what Carl was doing and was constantly weeding. Carl put the plant back into the earth. 'With the next one it will definitely work.' Carl thought. He took the next plant and dragged it carefully. Plop! Carl got angry. He only wanted to help the plant grow. Perhaps there was another way. Uncle Theodore told them to fertilize the plants so that they could grow better. But how could the leaves grow when the dung didn‘t touch them? It was clear: the cabbage grew so slowly because it stood the wrong way up. Busily he pulled out one plant after another and put them back into the earth upside down, so that the leaves were in the ground. He was very proud when he finished the work in his part of the field. All the plants were now planted, with the leaves in the earth. "Done!“ He was content with himself.

"What is that?“, Johnny frowned, "I am no real farmer, but that looks somehow backwards to me.“

"That‘s what you think", Carl said. "Now the dung reaches the leaves. This way the cabbage can grow quicker.“

"Aha. Are you sure? It sounds logical, but still doesn‘t look right.“

"Just let me do it“, Carl answered with determination. He started to pick plant after plant from Johnny‘s part of the field and put it back with the leaves down into the earth. Johnny stood there helpless. He didn‘t know enough about farming. Probably Carl was right. He let it happen. When all the plants were upside down, they went home.

"I will check it tomorrow morning, to see if it helped.“, Carl said amused.

The next morning Carl jumped happily to the field. It didn‘t bother him that the roots lay limp on the earth. He only wanted to know if the leaves had grown. He pulled one plant out. The leaves hung curled. Carl was horrified. What happened?

Why didn‘t they grow, but instead withered? He didn‘t understand. He dragged out another plant. This one was also withered. All the plants were withered!

He ran back to the house in desperation. "Johnny, a big catastrophe happened. Somebody must have poisoned our plants. They are all dead."
"What are you saying? Why are they poisoned?
"Yes, they are all dead. All the plants are withered and they have brown leaves. Somebody must have sprayed poison."
"Why would anyone have sprayed poison on our field?"
"I don‘t know. Perhaps someone was envious, because I had that super idea to put the leaves into the ground."
Slowly it began to dawn to Johnny, "Could it be that your idea wasn‘t as brilliant as you thought?"
"What do you mean?", Carl asked skeptically.
"Until yesterday, the plants were growing fine, but today, after you turned them around, they are now dead."
"You think it was not a good idea?"
"Looks that way."
"What are we going to do now?"
"The only thing we can do is to sow again."
"That is mean. I only meant well", Carl sulked.
"Nature doesn‘t care. She makes the rules. And we will not be able to change them. Good that it happened now, so we have at least the opportunity to sow again. It also could have been too late for that."
"I don‘t believe it! We need to start from the beginning?"

"Exactly." Encouragingly, he added: "Don't worry. You tried it and now you are wiser."
They started again with ploughing and sowing, weeding and watering. They were lucky. It wasn't too late. The crop started to sprout and soon the field was full of shining green leaves.

Some weeks passed by. Carl stood alone in their field. The cabbages in the fields around him were much bigger. They had lost precious time. Carl was angry at himself. It wasn't fun like this. He wanted to become famous with the biggest cabbages, and the cabbages were so small and only because he tried something. However, as Johnny said, he now was wiser. That was true. That wouldn't happen to him another time. He only caused trouble to Johnny. First the party and now the dead plants. He needed to fix it.

The Magic Potion

A wanderer walked by the field. He carried a big basket on his back. His sharp nose shivered, as if it smelled something. His eyes flashed and he said, "Good morning young man. Is that your field?"
Carl turned toward the wanderer, "Yes, it belongs to me and my brother."
"Ah, and what did you sow?"
"Mostly cabbages."
"That's perfect. I have something for you." He took the basket off his back and rummaged around. Carl got curious. He watched over the wanderer's shoulder. The guy dragged out a small bottle. It sparkled with exciting colors, like a

rainbow. Carl rubbed his eyes. Did the sun dazzle him? He never saw anything as wonderful as this. The wanderer whispered mysteriously into Carl‘s ear: "This is the best on the market. With this, your cabbage will become the biggest in the village.“ He made a meaningful pause. "And it works overnight.“ Carl's eyes grew wide. He would get the biggest cabbages in the village overnight?
"That‘s what this stuff can do?“, he asked.
"That‘s what this stuff can do! And because you are such a nice guy, I'll give you a super special price.“ The wanderer whispered the price into his ear. Carl was speechless. That really was a super special price. You couldn‘t do anything wrong with that. And when the fame came... If you watched him carefully, you could see small dollar-signs in his eyes. Carl saw himself already realizing all of his dreams. Without hesitating, he bought the bottle. The wanderer took his basket and went contentedly away.

Carl excitedly ran to Johnny. He held the bottle like a holy statue. "Johnny! I told you I would fix it.“ He told him about the wanderer and the magical growing potion. "Imagine, we don‘t need to wait until autumn. We can harvest tomorrow and then we can sow new seeds and harvest again.“ He jumped up and down.
"Are you serious?", said Johnny. "Don‘t you remember what Uncle Theodore used to tell us? We need to sow, cultivate and water and if we are lucky, we are able to harvest in the end. That‘s the law of nature. You don‘t really believe that this liquid helps? If it would, everybody would use it!“

"But the wanderer said it will work." Carl insisted. His eyes sparkled. He had an idea. "Fine, I will grow my own cabbage. We divide the field and see who is going to be more successful." Carl stood with folded arms in front of Johnny.
Johnny shook his head in disbelief. "If you think so." They split the field in two parts of the same size and shared the seed. In the end Carl made much ado about spreading his wonder-fluid on the field. He jumped up and down, danced pirouettes, waved his arms and mumbled strange things. He wanted to impress Johnny. "It only lacks your witch's broom!" Johnny snorted with laughter.
"You won't be laughing for long! By tomorrow you will see that I'll have the biggest cabbages!" Carl was out of puff.

They went home. Carl couldn't sleep that night. He was too excited. If it really would work, he would be a great mouse. Then he realized that he didn't ask the wanderer for his name. He didn't know how to find him if he needed more of the magical potion, "He will pass by again ." He calmed down.

After being awake all night, Carl jumped out of the bed with pleasant anticipation. With shivered whispers, he ran to the field. He almost stumbled as he arrived there. He was about to faint. He gasped for breath. In front of him lay a cabbage as big as a house! No, even as big as two houses! Big, green and thick. He shouted with joy. As quick as he could, he ran to the house. "Johnny, you must come immediately! It worked. You've

never seen something like this.“ Johnny came out the house. He couldn‘t believe it. He needed to see it with his own eyes. Both ran to the field and indeed: There lay a cabbage as big as... as... Johnny couldn't find the words.
"Hooray!“ Carl jumped around the cabbage. "I am rich! I am rich!“ Suddenly his whiskers touched the cabbage. There was a loud bang. With an ear deafening noise, the cabbage flew through the air and hit Carl. He couldn‘t jump aside quick enough. Shouting, Carl clawed at the cabbage.

They twirled through the air. From the left to the right, up and down and back again. They swirled like a balloon. When the air was out, the cabbage fell flabby on the earth and Carl was smothered by it.

Johnny rolled on the ground laughing. He almost couldn‘t breathe. Carl fought his way out of the cabbage leaves. He was glad to stand on solid ground again. He was stumbling. He looked disheveled and became agitated. "What a scam!“ The wanderer cheated him. He boiled with rage. How could he have been taken in by that guy?
He must admit that Johnny and Uncle Theodore were right. It only worked if you sowed, cultivated and watered and if you were lucky, you could harvest in the end. He stood small in front of Johnny. "You were right", he murmured, "as of now we do it like Uncle Theodore taught us.“
Johnny went quiet. "I am afraid it‘s too late. We cannot start again. We need to handle the situation as it is." Carl's ears drooped. Now they only had Johnny‘s cabbages left in the field.

Enemies Become Friends

Carl and Johnny removed the empty cabbage... and sowed again. They cultivated and watered their field. They weeded and spread manure. The cabbages and the grain grew slowly, but noticeably. Carl and Johnny enjoyed every day, because everything grew so nicely.

One morning, Carl and Johnny came to the field. The sun was just rising. The cabbages stood there in the field, shiny and green. Already from afar, they saw the birds. The birds came and jumped from one cabbage to the next, picking small pieces.
"Oh no!", Johnny shouted, "they will ruin everything!“

"We can't let that happen!", Carl answered. He ran and shouted and waved about with his arms. Johnny followed him. The birds flew up, alarmed.
"Go away!" Carl was frantic. How could they destroy their cabbages? They grew it so carefully and now these birds came and were destroying everything. The birds flew around the field and sat down at another corner of the cabbage field. This game went on several times.
"I have had enough", Carl snorted breathlessly, "I am getting the shotgun!"
"No, you can't!", Johnny said. He gasped for air. "You cannot shoot the birds! Normally they eat the bugs, which would eat into the cabbages. They are only hungry."
"And what do you think we shall do?"
"I don't know. What would Uncle Theodore have done?"
"I have no idea and we cannot ask him."
"Perhaps we can." The book came into Johnny's mind.
"You remember that the pages were empty? Nothing was written there", Carl asked in disbelief.
"Uncle Theodore said, when it is time, we will be able to see."
"Ok, if you think so." They ran to the house.
Fast as the wind, they rummaged out the book and flipped it open. Wildly they turned over page after page. They were still empty. No single letter in the whole book.
"Bloody hell!", swore Johnny and Carl at the same time.
"And now?", asked Johnny.
"I can still get the shotgun", answered Carl.

"They are only hungry. No, there must be another way."
"You have a better idea?"
"Let me think about it."
"Please think quickly, or our beautiful cabbages will be gone."
Johnny pondered a short while. "I have no idea. Perhaps we could talk with them."
"Talk? Should we invite them in for tea and cookies? Nonsense, I'll fetch the shotgun!" Carl stamped off.

Johnny went back to the field. The birds had not yet eaten away all the cabbages. Johnny shouted: "I think you are hungry, and you seem to like our cabbages. I completely understand, it really tastes fantastic. You are also really smart in evading our attacks and very persistent. "None of the birds reacted. He had an idea. "Nevertheless, I don't believe that you can finish the whole field." The smallest bird of the flock pricked his ears. He slipped past the others, who immediately stopped picking. The small bird fluffed up his feathers and asked, "And why shouldn't we finish the whole field?"
"Because in the next two minutes my brother will be here with a shotgun."
"What does he want with a shotgun?"
"In the best case, he will chase you away."
"And in the worst?"
"In the worst case, your feathers will get holes."
The first bird swallowed and the others' eyes widened.
"That will definitely hurt", he said.
Johnny nodded.

"But we are so hungry", the bird pleaded.
"I do understand. I don't want you to starve. How would it be..." Johnny could't finish his sentence.

A troop of marching little black beetles came up to them. Left, two, three, four, left, two, three, four... Determined, they steered straight to the field. They had only eyes for the cabbages. Johnny wasn't sure, but it looked as if every beetle held a knife in his right hand and in the left hand a fork. Oh no, he thought, these are the greedy cabbage beetles. Within a few seconds these bugs could scoff down huge cabbage fields. First the birds and now the bugs. They were lost! He had little hope, that the cabbage was to be rescued. He pulled himself together and asked: "What are you about to do?"

The first beetle sat up: "We are going to eat the cabbages."
"Oh, no you don't!", Johnny shouted out angrily.
"And who will stop us?"
"My brother and I!"
"Ho-hum", replied the beetle and looked disdainfully. The beetles marched on.
"And us", joined in the first bird. The flock moved closer and pounced. The beetles looked to Johnny and then to the birds. Very determined they stood in front of him, "So, you and your brother cannot stop us. Before you can say 'cabbage-stew', the cabbages will be already eaten. The birds however are a very unattractive issue." He seemed to ponder and then he said: "Fellows, let's go. "The troop struck a new direction and moved on.
As quickly as they came, they disappeared. Johnny took a deep breath. He had almost forgot to breathe. This time it worked out well. He plopped down on his back.
"Thank you for your help!"
"You helped us, too. You warned us about your brother. And we dislike those bugs. Wherever they appear, nothing's left over. For anybody."
"What about splitting the field. You get a piece only for you and the rest is for Carl and myself. Then everybody has their own cabbages. Nobody will have to starve. Carl doesn't need to shoot you and we won't see the beetles again."
They agreed and everybody got what they needed.

The Mice Pull Together

The summer came. The days got longer and the temperature rose. The sun burnt stronger every day. Carl and Johnny had trouble watering the fields enough. It was only a matter of time until the ditches around the fields dried out. Until now, they didn't have a long way to go with their watering cans. If the ditches dried out, they would have to walk to the stream and this was far away and difficult to reach. All the other farmers also fought with the water shortage. Carl and Johnny ran as quickly as they could, in every hand a watering can, but they had barely spread the water before it was already drained away. Totally exhausted, Johnny stopped.

"We simply cannot water everything."

"What shall we do?", Carl asked.

"I don't know. I only know that we will lose everything if we go on like this."

"You mean, we should abandon a part of the harvest? That is out of the question! We worked too hard and what should we live on during the winter?"

"Suit yourself", Johnny backed down. So, they continued running, until the sunset allowed them a little break. In the evening the farmers all went home exhausted.

Carl lay in his bed. He was thinking. He knew the weather was only going to stay hot and dry. Johnny was right, they couldn't do it alone. If they didn't want to lose the whole harvest, they had to come up with something. But what? There must be a solution. If they only had more people. By no means did he want to give up.

Carl woke up early. The sun was forgiving today, but it wouldn't take long until it would burn down

again, without mercy. There was gloom at breakfast. It seemed as if they would lose the fight against the heat.
"We need help", Carl mumbled.
"That's what I say, but where do we get it from?"
"Perhaps the other farmers have some ideas."
"They have nothing to do, but to carry the water around like idiots."
"Then we need to think about it all together. I'll invite the farmers."
Johnny agreed. It was better than doing nothing.

Half an hour later, all of the farmer-mice were sitting in Carl and Johnny's living room. Everybody was at a loss. There were a lot of dry summers in Happiness, but somehow they always found a solution so that the plants didn't shrivel. They had never before known such a dry season. There were a few farmers that didn't suffer as much. Their fields were located near the stream. They also came, because they cared about their friends and neighbors.
Together, they thought about a solution. There were a lot of proposals that couldn't be realized. After a lot of back and forth, the oldest mouse said: "We should see how we can keep the damage as small as possible, how we could support one another."
"Maybe we could work together with the irrigation", one mouse proposed. "Today one field and tomorrow the other."
"But then the first field will be already dried out the following day."
"We all need to care about one field all together", another mouse suggested.

Now the mice were all talking at once.
"And which field will we take? What about the other fields?"
"We have the best cabbage and we let it dry out?"
"Will there remain enough for everybody?"

All the time, Carl sat quietly in a corner. Now he barged in: "Enough! There must be another solution. We have to find a way to water all the fields." He came up with an idea. "We need a machine."
"A machine?"
"What do you mean?"
"We have always made it without that modern stuff."
Johnny piped up, "Yes, and now we are failing to do it. Perhaps the time has come for something new."
"We don't have a clue about machines."
"You think because you come from the big town that you know how things work better?"
"We only want to rescue the harvest", Johnny replied. "I am also clueless about machines. But something will come to mind."
The mice were doubtful. At last, the oldest said: "We don't have any choice. The circumstances have changed, so we need to change something. What do you suggest?"
"We need to build something that will transport the water from the stream to the fields."
"What are you thinking about?"
"Near the stream is a mill. With that, we could bail the water out of the stream."
"The mill is too far away from the fields."

"That's true. Then, we need to build our own mill",
Carl said.
"How?"
"Good question. We need a wheel and something that activates it."
"I have an old bicycle!", one mouse chipped in.
"Yes, and we fix some mugs on the bike with which to bail the water", suggested Johnny.

Now, the mice started to move. Everybody thought about how they could contribute. Carl listened carefully. He started to draw a draft. There were two other mice who supported him. Quickly, it became clear what they needed. Contentedly, they watched the drawing of their new water transport machine. Carl gave instructions on who should bring what. Even the kids were sent out to bring their colored windmills. They grumbled and didn't want to hand them over. Johnny said quietly: "We need your windmills to help our friends, so please fetch them." The mice-kids started to run.

After a short while, a big heap of all the needed stuff piled up in the middle of the courtyard. There were big and small hoses, a bicycle, cans, a cone, trunks, planks, an old cartwheel, nails, rubber gloves, tights, straws and the kids' windmills.

Carl explained the water transport machine. He asked every mouse what they could do well and then he gave them a task. Even the kids helped out. They got to stick the straw together into long chains. One group had to go on watering the fields with the watering cans. Eagerly, everyone got to work.

They were hammering, sawing, cutting and putting parts together. They positioned the big cartwheel near the stream, after they had fixed the cans. The wheel was powered by the bicycle. They removed the inner tube and put the knotted tights through from the back-wheel of the bicycle to the hub of the cartwheel. A mouse sat on the bicycle and pedaled. The cans bailed the water from one side, out of the stream and on the other side, the water was tilted into the cone. The big hose was fixed to the cone. The water ran through the hose into the gloves. The gloves had small holes in the fingers. In these holes were the kids' straw-chains.

The mice put the straw-chains on crutches across the fields. At the end, the children's windmills stood angular to the ground. The water ran on the mills, activated by the wind and spread the water far over the field.

Everybody was happy when they saw the water running and the fields were watered with almost no effort. The mice were giddy with pleasure and they relaxed. Now they only needed to take turns to drive the bicycle and check the hose regularly. They made a plan for that. Day after day, they watered the fields with the water transport machine. They averted the catastrophe as they worked together. Everyone contributed to the project.

The Courageous Idea

Slowly, autumn came. The days turned shorter and colder. The cabbage stood full and green in the fields. It was the time of harvesting.
The mice knew that they needed to hurry up. It mustn't become too cold. If the cabbage froze, the harvest would be spoiled. In the meantime, they came together as a big community and supported one another during the harvest.

Every night, the temperature fell lower. Finally, the thermometer showed minus degrees. The mice got anxious about that. Nobody reckoned such an early start to the coldness. It seemed as if they would lose the harvest. In the summer, they had overcome the dryness and the next catastrophe now lurked. They rushed as much as they could, but the coldness was quicker. It looked like they could only harvest for two more days. After this, the rest would be lost.

In the evening, Carl and Johnny sat in front of the oven. They sat there quietly, deep in thought. Carl broke the silence first: "I don‘t want to go back into town!“

"What makes you think we'll have to?“

"If we don‘t have enough food, we will need to return to the city. Then, we will have to collect scraps again. I don‘t want to do that. I want to stay here. Here, we have real friends and a real job. And we can't get such delicious cabbage in the city.“

"We are not yet as far as that. We‘ll find a solution.“

At this moment, the door-bell rang. All the mice of the village stood in front of the door. Carl and Johnny let them in.

"We thought we should find a solution, all together again.“

"Yes, in the summer it worked out well.“ The mice each took places around the oven and planned.

"Could we build a machine again?“, asked one mouse.

"That wouldn't work. The cabbage must be harvested by hand. If not, it will be destroyed“, answered another mouse.

"And could we cover it?“

"That wouldn’t help. The ground is already too cold.“

"If we don‘t come up with something, we will lose half of the cabbages“, the oldest mouse said. "The rest would not be strong enough to survive the winter."

"The beautiful cabbages. The best in the world and now it freezes", lamented one mouse.

Carl pricked his ears. The whole time, he had the impression that he had overlooked something, as if the solution was right in front of his nose. Suddenly, it came into his mind. Wasn't he just thinking why he didn't want to go back into town? And now they talked about the best cabbages in the world.

"I have the solution!", he shouted out. "Do you know that they don't have our cabbages in the town?"

"Yes, of course. You can only get it here."

"And that's the reason why we will sell it in town for a lot of money."

The mice watched him with big eyes.

"What do you mean?"

"Why should anyone buy our cabbages?"

Carl was totally excited. "Because it's the best! You said it !"

For one moment, everyone was completely silent.

"Our cabbage really tastes the best."

"Yes, and it doesn't smell when you cook it."

"And it doesn't give you gas", beeped one mouse, ashamed, from the back.

"It also makes other people happy." Everybody laughed and suddenly they were all excited.

"You mean, we accept that one part of our cabbage freezes? And we sell the rest in the city? Do you think we will earn enough for all of us?", the oldest mouse addressed Carl.

"Yes, of course! For good products, people pay good money. With the goodness of our cabbages, nothing can go wrong." He paused.
"The Happi-Cabbage makes you and your beloved happy."
The mice applauded.
Johnny was skeptical. "What if it doesn't work? If it's not as easy as you think?" Carl saw the mice's courage waiver.
"I have no doubt that it will work out well. We must dare do it. We have no other choice. If we hold on together, we will make it!"
"We could add some of our favorite recipes", one of the mice thought loudly.
"Good idea."
"And we could paint colorful pictures", the children peeped.
"Yes, we could create nice flyers. With pictures of Happiness and the best recipes. Then all the mice in town will know where the cabbage comes from and how they could cook great dishes from it", reflected Carl.
"We could also tell a story about the life of a head of a cabbage, what it has experienced this year until it found its way to town."

Everybody was enthusiastic. It was a done deal. They arranged duties and everyone started with eagerness. From time to time, they lost heart when they found a ruined cabbage. Carl brightened them up immediately. They mustn't give up. They had to harvest as much as possible. That he himself had doubts at times, he didn't tell them. It must work.

The mice cut the cabbage and packed them in boxes. Every cabbage got a colorful booklet. They stacked the boxes on Uncle Theodore‘s horse-drawn buggy and Carl drove into town. He was all on edge with what he could expect. He hadn’t done this before. He also had no clue where to start. The only clear thing was, that he had to sell the cabbages.

Three days passed by. The mice in Happiness fluttered. Johnny gave them work. Nobody should be worried about the situation. In the evening of the third day, Carl returned. The mice saw him arriving from far away. They were excited and couldn‘t wait for his arrival. When he entered the courtyard, they surrounded the cart.
Carl pulled a long face. It went silent. The mice stopped breathing.
"It didn‘t work?“, worried the oldest.
Suddenly Carl was all smiles and he threw bundles of money into the crowd, "It worked! Much better than I expected.“ Everyone celebrated. The mice pulled Carl from the cart and carried him, singing loudly, through the whole village. Everybody was relieved that they had succeeded. They even found another world. Thanks to the early winter and Carl‘s courage.

The mice spontaneously prepared a big feast. They made a fire and everyone brought something to eat. The children made bread on a stick. All were happy, and they laughed and danced. A heavy burden had fallen off their shoulders. They talked about their success and almost couldn‘t believe what happened. They were all glad to live in Happiness, the place where nobody could harm them.

The Secret of Happiness

Carl and Johnny stood aside. Johnny put his arms around Carl: "I am very proud of you my brother. You rescued the village with your courage and your ideas."

"We did that all together. You believed in us as well, which made it possible", Carl said. They looked to the others.

"That was a really exciting year", said Carl.

"That's true. No year before that was as exciting as this. We experienced a lot. It was not always easy, but I am glad to be here."

"It's a pity that Uncle Theodore cannot see how far we've come", sighed Carl.
"We were lucky that Uncle Theodore invited us to come here."
"Yes, he taught us a lot."
"Nevertheless, I still don't understand the meaning of the empty book. Why isn't there anything written there?", asked Carl.
Johnny thought for a short while. "I ask myself if it would have really helped us. Perhaps it only means that you cannot read experiences. We need to live through experiences."
Carl watched the stars in the sky. "All mice in the world should have such a good life as we have."
Johnny agreed. For one moment they hung on their own thoughts.
Suddenly, Johnny said: "How would it be if we wrote everything down, what we have learned so far, for all the mice who don't have an Uncle Theodore?"
Carl was immediately excited. "Yes, then they could also learn how to grow the best cabbage. They could come to Happiness and we will show them."
"We will get to know many, many mice and could also learn a lot."
"Everybody brings his experiences and all of that will be written in the book."
"Perhaps, also mice from Africa, America and Asia will join us."
"Yes, we will all become friends and then no mouse on this earth will ever be alone, or starve."
"That's what we are going to do." They laughed.
That night, they started to write. They wrote and wrote until they fell asleep over the book. When

they woke up the next morning, they had written down all that they had learned.

Outside on the yard, carriages came. They heard loud voices. The mice-brothers stretched and moved drowsily to the door. They had hardly opened the door when the popping of flashbulbs flashed across the courtyard. There were about 20 mice with cameras hoping to shoot a picture of Carl and Johnny.

***

Luke is totally excited. "Carl really became famous then? Just as he wanted to?“ His grandpa shrugs his shoulders: "What do you think?“
"They wanted to take pictures of him! I am sure that they were reporters from the newspapers!“ Luke is completely captured by the story. "Carl succeeded. Even though they didn't have any money, he never gave up. Even though it was not easy, and he made many mistakes, he always believed in his dream.“ His grandpa nods. Luke asks: "Grandpa, does this book really exist?“
"Of course.“

Luke's eyes are getting bigger. "Really? Do you have that book?“
His grandpa lifts him up off his lap and stands up. He goes to his bag, which he always carries around, and opens it. He delves into it and takes out a thick leather-bound book. Luke stared at him. His grandpa passes him the book. Luke takes it and opens it carefully.

There, it is written:

Everything starts with a dream.

You need to treat the cow you want to milk very well.

As a farmer, you shouldn't eat your seed.

Cabbage doesn't grow faster when you pull on it.

Be mindful of risks.

Your enemies could become your friends.

Never give up, no matter what happens.

Be willing to try new experiences.

Together, you are stronger.

In every crisis, there is a golden opportunity.

Have the courage to take risks.

Make your own experiences.

Share your knowledge with others.

***

Sandra Jantzen
our author is from Hamburg. With her peaceful prose, she conjures vivid pictures into the hearts of readers. Playfully, she awakens the imagination of young and old. As a ghostwriter, she helps people to find the words that open and touch the heart.
As a coach and trainer she accompanies people on their way to freedom and self-expression. Her big dream is to create a training farm: a place where people meet, develop and grow. Sandra already has two Galloway cows, Emily and Adrian, ready to start at the training farm.

Robert Jansen
is a farmer, coach and international speaker. Corporations hire this father of four for his 30 years of experience as a highly successful entrepreneur. He earned his living with his hugely popular patented product Jaroma®-Kohl, a special cabbage. Robert Jansen

combines profound insights of nature with modern management strategies. In his book „Vergiss das Verkaufen“ (Forget about Selling), he talks about the secret of endearing communication. With his company, he transformed his passion into his profession. He supports people in finding their own game and guiding them to win.
www.jaro-peoplegrowers.com

Andrea Ludwig
is a coach and trainer and lives in Ibiza. From there, she travels the world to pass on her knowledge to corporations and private clients. With her organizing ability Andrea coordinates teams, keeping them united and playing for one another. She ensures the completion of tasks and achieves results. Her mission is to support people in discovering and reaching their dreams, their potentials and their goals.
www.poweraufdenpunkt.de
www.kickyourass.eu

All illustrations drawn by Dieter Hermenau. www.hermenaucartoons.de

25478150R20032

Made in the USA
Charleston, SC
30 December 2013